RHYMING FUN

Edited By Roseanna Caswell

First published in Great Britain in 2022 by:

YoungWriters®
Est. 1991

Young Writers
Remus House
Coltsfoot Drive
Peterborough
PE2 9BF
Telephone: 01733 890066
Website: www.youngwriters.co.uk

Printed and bound in the UK by BookPrintingUK
Website: www.bookprintinguk.com
YB0498T

FOREWORD

For Young Writers' latest competition This Is Me,
we asked primary school pupils to look inside
themselves, to think about what makes them unique,
and then write a poem about it! They rose to the
challenge magnificently and the result is this fantastic
collection of poems in a variety of poetic styles.

Here at Young Writers our aim is to encourage creativity
in children and to inspire a love of the written word, so
it's great to get such an amazing response, with some
absolutely fantastic poems. It's important for children to
focus on and celebrate themselves and this competition
allowed them to write freely and honestly, celebrating
what makes them great, expressing their hopes and
fears, or simply writing about their favourite things.
This Is Me gave them the power of words. The result
is a collection of inspirational and moving poems that
also showcase their creativity and writing ability.

I'd like to congratulate all the young poets
in this anthology, I hope this inspires them
to continue with their creative writing.

CONTENTS

Melrose At The Ladies College, St Peter Port

Sienna Wallen (11)	45

New Row Primary School, Castledawson

Grace Mulholland (8)	47
Eliana Coleman (9)	48
Daniel Gribbin (9)	49
Shann Bradley (8)	50
Ellie Bigger (8)	51
Tomas Cleary (8)	52
Sophia McMullan (8)	53
Senan Lupari (8)	54
Leo Graham (9)	55
Nicola Szeliga (9)	56
Emily Young (9)	57
Thomas Gribbin (9)	58
Josh Skelly (8)	59
Charlotte Bothwell (8)	60
Rafferty Hassan (9)	61
Phelim Kealey (8)	62
Noah Gribbin (9)	63
Juliette Konkiewicz (8)	64
Sean Lavery (8)	65
Michael McLarnon (8)	66
Senan Hughes (8)	67
Chloe Doherty (8)	68
Daire McErlean (8)	69
Saoirse Martin (9)	70
Caolan Fitzsimons (9)	71
Conan Lagan (8)	72
Cathal Gallagher (8)	73
Eabha Totten (8)	74
Kathryn McLaughlin (8)	75
Elliot Smyth (8)	76
Carol Ferris (9)	77

Oystermouth Primary School, Mumbles

Megan Pyke (10)	78
Charlie	79
Indi Belton (10)	80
Meghan Clift (10)	81
Samuel Harris (9)	82
Ned Calder (9)	83
Alfred Ronnie Williams (9)	84
Daisy Spatuzzi (9)	85
Ellen Curley (9)	86
Erin Porter (10)	87
Eryn Harwood (9)	88
Maia Hayward (10)	89
Elsie Brain (9)	90
Aisha Keogh (10)	91
Pietro Da Silva (9)	92
Joshua Alkarnaz (9)	93
Dylan Ravitz (9)	94
Seren James (10)	95
Olivia Kenna (11)	96
Emily-Rose Walker (9)	97
Elin Koscian (10)	98
Elijah Coughan (9)	99
Grayson Thomas (9)	100
Ted Thomas (9)	101
Louie Beck (9)	102
Caitlin Vaughan (9)	103
Maxwell Fuller (10)	104
Ella Jardine	105
Cai Clement (10)	106
Bodhi Maddern Nixon (10)	107
Louis Franklin (11)	108
Ben Smith (9)	109
Anjali Munnangi (10)	110
Harri Davies (9)	111
Bethan Lewis (9)	112
Ioan Jones (11)	113
James Dumpleton	114
Elliott	115
Aeron Wilson Whitcombe	116
Orla Richards (9)	117
Nell Brain	118

Sofia Sewell Hunter (10) 119
Lyla Jonsson (11) 120
Ethan (10) 121
Olivia B 122
Lex Morgan (9) 123
Bella Morgan (11) 124

Pimlico Academy, Westminster

Ruth Kaputa (11) 125

Richmond Avenue Primary School, Shoeburyness

Eriona Ahmeti 126
Reuben Mayne (8) 127
Eliot Bodacz (7) 128
Evie Shepherd (7) 129
Millie (7) 130
Matilda Rutt (7) 131
Rosemary Palmer (8) 132
Amy Stoner (8) 133
Isla Divall (7) 134
Scarlett Wood (7) 135
Austin Higgins (7) 136
Jessica Jackson (7) 137
Liberty Hall (7) 138
Maisie Giles (7) 139
Thomas Bannister (7) 140
Evie Saville (7) 141
Seth Brown (7) 142
Reuben Clark (7) 143
Matilda White (7) 144
Lily Dickenson (7) 145
Olivia Tofts (7) 146
Angus Gavin (8) 147
Gabrielle Ellis (7) 148
Mia Takacs (7) 149
Sebastian Quayle (7) 150
Zakk Edwards (8) 151
Sidney Tuffin (7) 152
Jack Conner (7) 153
Lucas Hughes (7) 154
Liam Williams (7) 155

Riley Caron (7) 156
Riley-Rae Dadds (7) 157
Arianna Causova (7) 158

The St Teresa Catholic Primary School, Dagenham

David Gabor (8) 159
Shreya Solan (8) 160
Johann Joseph (8) 162
Sofia Takacs (8) 164
Francis Nnaike (9) 165
Sarah Lalu (8) 166
Marcus Icaro (8) 167
Rochelle Itonga (8) 168
Isla Robertson (8) 169
Andreja Andreja (8) 170
Tommy Grote 171
Youjin Son (8) 172

The Welbourn CE Primary School, Welbourn

Dan Bull (10) 173
George K (9) 174
Lottie Bull (10) 176
Finlay G (9) 178
Cassius M (10) 180
Joe Miller (10) 181
Elise G (10) 182
Evie Batchelor (10) 183
Isla W (10) 184
Maxi M (9) 185

Totternhoe CE Academy, Totternhoe

Eliza Barford (8) 186
Holly Boiteux-Buchanan (8) 187
Delphi Joslyn-Walker (8) 188
Madison Darvell (8) 189
Lylah Rose Nash (8) 190

Worth Valley Primary School, Keighley

Carson Rigby (7)	191
Lucie Gill (7)	192
Anne Roberts (7)	193
Poppie-Jae Antenbring (8)	194
Evah Smith (7)	195
Terrell Howell (7)	196
Lucas Bogle (7)	197
Joseph Batt (7)	198
Darcy Ingham (7)	199
Mylie Jae Montgomery (7)	200
Elijah Moorby-Byrne (7)	201
Dylan Richmond (7)	202
Keira-Jade Feather (7)	203
Jenson Greenwood (7)	204

THE POEMS

My Cat

My cat is really cute and curious
He sometimes bites you when you hurt him
He bites me but not all the time
When he bites me, it makes me sad and cry
But my mom is kind
She cheers me up to make me feel happy
And she scares the cat away
My cat is really messy with his food
And he doesn't eat it all
He likes playing with his toy bird
At night, he never sleeps
But in the day he sleeps.

Elizabeth Kyrychenko (7)
ACS International School, Cobham

Me And Ted

I went to bed and I said
My ted is dead from his head
His name is Fred and I miss him snoring
I am kind and I find coins and they're gold
like my ted
I'm smart and I have a heart and I fart
I get mad and sad and bad and I like sports
and forts
I would like a horse and I play golf on a
golf course.

Suvi Sidhu (7)
ACS International School, Cobham

Love

Love grows inside the heart
If you're scared or in fear
It never happens if I'm here
Love does not come from the outside
It comes from the inside
Love is all that matters to me and you!

Isabella Pelliccia (8)
ACS International School, Cobham

Stitch

He is soft
He is cute and warm
I love him
So does Lelowe
You can see him
Somewhere fun you can go
His name starts with a 'S'
Can you guess?

Answer: Stitch.

Anna Ford (7)
ACS International School, Cobham

Me

M y unicorns

A bsolutely great at maths

T reasure

I maginative

L over of unicorns

D ancer

A bsolutely fabulous.

Matilda Rymarczyk (9)

ACS International School, Cobham

Autumn

A s I was sitting
U nder a tree, looking at
T he falling leaves, I looked
U p and thought about how
M uch I love
N ature.

Lillian Essaye (8)
ACS International School, Cobham

Things That Make Me, Me

I dream about the ocean
That's where I like to be.
My Gramma is my happy place
And that is a side of me.

Emily Hoy (7)
ACS International School, Cobham

My Smile

My smile goes 1,000 miles
It brightens my day
In the bay
And it is here to stay!

Omar Jabshah (7)
ACS International School, Cobham

My Life

Sunny seaside walks with my dog
Hang*I*ng out with friends
Ar*E* the things I like to do, but
Nothing makes me happier than dancing around
To the latest TikTok tre*N*ds
Activities I love include swimming, karate and
football, which I definitely recommend.

Sienna Moores (11)

Berrow CE Primary School, Berrow

All About Millie

M is for most kind
I is for interested
L is for loving
L is for living
I is for incredible
E is for educational.

Millie Allen (10)
Berrow CE Primary School, Berrow

Keira, This Is Me

My friends like who I am, kind and caring
The teachers think I am very helpful
I am like the jam inside a cake
My friends think that is really great
Caring about the people in my life, dead or alive
My heart lays upon everyone in my life.

Keira Johannes (10)
Eye CE Primary School, Eye

I Am... Jess

A cinquain poem

Jessie
Monkey crazy
I like monkeys, they're cute
Laughing, dancing, modelling, sing
Monkey!

Jessica Lenihan (11)
Eye CE Primary School, Eye

Megan

A cinquain poem

Megan
Likes marshmallows
Plays football all the time
I only eat pasta and cheese
Good food.

Megan Kirby (11)
Eye CE Primary School, Eye

This Is Me, James

A cinquain poem

James Bil
Funny, crazy
Class clown, always laughing
Wants to be a good mechanic
Tigers.

James Bilton (11)
Eye CE Primary School, Eye

This Is Me

A cinquain poem

Hollie
Funny and kind
Shimmering and shiny
Loves to dance and loves to perform
Tigers.

Hollie Childs (10)
Eye CE Primary School, Eye

Logan

A cinquain poem

Logan
Loves to play games
Coding is the best game
Great designer, so creative
Tigers.

Logan Giles (10)
Eye CE Primary School, Eye

Peter

A cinquain poem

Peter
Bright, crazy, fun
Class clown, always laughing
Wants to be a comedian
Tiger.

Peter Stoneman (10)
Eye CE Primary School, Eye

Finley

A cinquain poem

Finley
Funny, quiet
Class clown, always quiet
I want to be a great artist
Lions.

Finley Nolan (10)
Eye CE Primary School, Eye

Georgia! This Is Me

A cinquain poem

Georgia
Bacon crazy
Class clown and weird
I will be an actress soon, yay!
Funny.

Georgia Kerry (11)
Eye CE Primary School, Eye

Henry

A cinquain poem

Henry
Unique, crazy
Wants to be a pianist
Curious, bright and talkative
Lions.

Henry Cavender (10)
Eye CE Primary School, Eye

All About Amber

A cinquain poem

Amber
Confident, fun
Always has ideas
Has fun when I am with my friends
Happy.

Amber Kaur (10)

Eye CE Primary School, Eye

This Is Me, Ruby

A cinquain poem

Ruby
Loving, caring
Always nice to my friends
Never betray my BFFs
Tiger.

Ruby Parker (10)
Eye CE Primary School, Eye

This Is Me, Izzy

A cinquain poem

Izzy
Fashionable
Isabella likes food
Izzy wants to be a teacher
Tigers.

Isabella Deegan (10)
Eye CE Primary School, Eye

All About Me

I love animals and I'd like to see an elephant herd
Although I'd like to be a bird
I'd zoom through the sky
Way up high
As I listen to the sounds below
I love baby toys that once were mine
But I'm too old for them as I'm nine
I love riding my little bike
And going with Cubs on a hike
I'm fascinated by art
From the very start
Of my phenomenal life.

Alexis Cover (9)
Grove Primary School, Carlton Colville

My Life

My name is Bella and I like blue
Maybe you do too
Let me ask about you
I heard about you
You sound funny and friendly too
I came up with a rhyme for you
Roses are red
Violets are blue
They are bright just like you.

Isabella Rudder (10)
Grove Primary School, Carlton Colville

Happy Girl

There was a young girl
That loved to dance and twirl
She was always happy

With long golden hair
And always wanting to share
She was always happy

I'm so lucky she is my friend
I hope it never ends.

Isla Jefferson (7)
Grove Primary School, Carlton Colville

Great Things About Me

I am Eliza.
I am eight.
Here are some reasons why I am great:
I have big curly hair
And with my friends, I always share.
I love nature.
My favourite colour is green.
I am always kind but never mean.
I love my cats, Cleo, Oreo and Skye,
Like me in my gymnastics class, they jump very high.
I love my mum and when we have fun,
She makes my heart beat like a drum.
I hope you like my poem,
And that my personality is showing.

Eliza Boateng (8)
Marden Vale Academy, Calne

Me And My Friend

B est friends forever, we love being together, my friend, Summer

L aughing and playing, running and climbing, my friend, Summer

U nder the trees, we made secret dens as neighbours together, my friend, Summer

E very Friday night, we turned on the light to eat fish and chips, my friend, Summer

B efore I know it, Summer was moving. I was very sad, my friend, Summer

E very day, we made the most of being together before she left for Australia, my friend, Summer

L ooking for Summer and she is not there, my friend, Summer

L ove you, Summer, you were the best, my friend, Summer

E very night, I'm waiting for you, my friend, Summer.

Bluebelle Barlow (9)

Margaretting CE (VC) Primary School, Margaretting

My Christmas

I run to my mother to give her a hug,
I get in the car and drive far away,
I see snow coming down,
Christmas trees peeping through windows
I see the postman with a jolly smile,
I can feel the lovely heated seat
I can still see the snow coming down
I smell lovely mince pies waiting for me on the side
I love home, I love home
The fire, the Christmas tree, the things I love
I smell a Christmas-scented candle
I hear a robin singing a lovely song
I love Christmas!
It is the best time of year
Father Christmas filling stockings
Giving red and gold presents
Lovely blanket over you.
Home sweet home!

Freddie Scales (11)
Margaretting CE (VC) Primary School, Margaretting

Ginger And Proud

I am ginger and proud
Because I stand out from the crowd
My hair makes me unique
But it doesn't make me a freak
Ginge is my name to my friends and family
People try to bully me but that just makes
them silly
Don't judge a book by its cover
Just because I'm ginger, I'm still like any other
If you give me a chance, you will see I'm a
good friend
I'll stick with you until the end
So next time you see me, don't judge me by
my hair
Show me respect and show me you care
So when you see me standing out from the crowd
Always remember I'm ginger and proud.

Bobby Crouch (9)
Margaretting CE (VC) Primary School, Margaretting

All My Animals

A ll my animals can be a bit devious but I look after them and love them

N ow I've got four chickens, one of them is new and the other three don't like it

I n my house, it's a bit crazy. We have so many pets. Everywhere I look there's one

M ost of my pets are lizards, I've got three bearded dragons and one gecko

A nd so many more to come. I'm not going to tell you all of them though

L ots of animals, lots and lots. Some people might say it's a zoo

S ome people might not like it but I do. I think a family should have lots of animals.

Elsie Smith (9)

Margaretting CE (VC) Primary School, Margaretting

The Recipe Of Me

First mix in the joy and smiles
Then add in the care
A dash of the sun will add some fun
Now let's move on to the hair

A good helping of red was added to my locks
But you can choose pink or blue
Either of these colours will do just fine
It's utterly up to you

Moving on to the face, a smidge of blue
Will make my eyes stand out
A sprinkle of freckles across my nose
You'll know it's me, no doubt

Pour in a Mum
A dollop of Dad
And a pinch of little brother
All these ingredients in this recipe
Must be combined together.

Ava-Jean Barham (10)
Margaretting CE (VC) Primary School, Margaretting

All About Me And What I Love

My name is Grace
My favourite colour is blue
I don't mind a bit of purple and orange too
I'm nine years old and I have a little puppy
Her name is Coco and she's very fluffy
My little puppy, she's very funny
She runs in circles and even in streams
She has a basket of toys
But still finds something in the garden to destroy
Our garden is full of holes
It looks like we've had a mole
I help fill up the holes
She's like a little monkey.

Grace Davies (9)
Margaretting CE (VC) Primary School, Margaretting

All About My Life

I'm Hannah and I have a dog called Dash
He is fast like the Flash
My brother, called Daniel, likes to play football
I like to play Barbies all day
Even though I'm nine
I don't really care what people say
Because it's my doll and I do it my way
Making things is my hobby
Soup? Nah, it's kind of sloppy
Watch TV or play Roblox all day
I want my own room
I share with my brother
Please, please, please
Never mind, don't bother.

Hannah Ogundele (9)
Margaretting CE (VC) Primary School, Margaretting

Bessie

B eing me, young and free, blonde and curly, can't you see?

E legant, polite, big feet, tall height, absolutely loving life, doing what's right

S ummer's my fave, winter's next, drawing pictures, typing texts

S ister to Joe, sister to Clark, caring for each other, daylight to dark

I nspiration, Mother and Father, celebs on TV, must try harder

E nd of the day, you see what you see, but look to my inside, to really see me!

Bessie Burns (10)

Margaretting CE (VC) Primary School, Margaretting

The Things I Like

My name is Joseph, Joseph Lowe
I run real fast and walk real slow
I have one brother and a sister too
Here are the things I like to do
Riding my bike is very fun
In the park and in the sun
Eating Turkish, stirfry too
Here are some things I like to do
Playing on my iPad, swimming in the pool
I think these things are really cool
I'm nine years old and my birthday is in November
I love roast dinners, just remember.

Joseph Adam Lowe (9)
Margaretting CE (VC) Primary School, Margaretting

Noah Craig

N ever going to forget joining Margaretting

O verwhelmed and nervous as I walked through the gate

A lways hoping to make a new mate

H appy and excited about my day ahead

C aring and kind is what I am

R eady to learn and take on a new term

A n amazing time I have had

I now love school and don't want it to end

G oing up to seniors next year, for my next adventure.

Noah Embery (10)
Margaretting CE (VC) Primary School, Margaretting

Me

E vie is my lovely name
V ery funny and full of flames
I love interior design
E njoying games with friends of mine

B londe, blue-eyed and tall
E very time I hit the tennis ball
L earning, I find cool
L oving it in the swimming pool
O nly deep down I would know
Y ou are invited to come with my flow.

Evie Belloy (9)
Margaretting CE (VC) Primary School, Margaretting

This Is Me

If the world was owned by me
I would let the elephants roam free
I would walk by their side at night
Under the stars and the moonlight

I'm forever happy with glee
To be surrounded by my family
They all think I'm nice and funny
I wouldn't change them for love or money.

Evie Warren (9)
Margaretting CE (VC) Primary School, Margaretting

All About Oscar

O perating on animals is what I want to do

S aving them to make them feel brand new

C aring for animals makes me proud and happy

A vet is what I really want to be because animals make me smile with glee

R eptiles, mammals, amphibians and birds all need care.

Oscar Groves (10)

Margaretting CE (VC) Primary School, Margaretting

Just Like Me

The sun is bright, just like me
A cheetah is lively, just like me
A bear is brave, just like me
Flowers are beautiful, just like me
A bird is free, just like me
The leaves are changing, just like me
Twigs are random, just like me
And nature is wild, just like me.

Holly Jones (9)
Margaretting CE (VC) Primary School, Margaretting

About Me, Max Wu

M aths is my favourite subject
A lphabet won't bring me joy
X mas tree is taller than me

W hat I want is a wonderful toy
U nforgettable memories in Hong Kong keeps me happy all day long.

King Yui Wu (9)
Margaretting CE (VC) Primary School, Margaretting

Mallo

M y dog, Mallo

A nd he is really sweet

L ove him all you can and he will love you back

L earn from him

O bviously the best Dalmatian in the world.

Laila Williams (10)

Margaretting CE (VC) Primary School, Margaretting

Ellie

E njoying fun and friends
L earning never ends
L aughing and loving
I magination is true
E veryone's amazing!

Ellie Hunter (9)
Margaretting CE (VC) Primary School, Margaretting

Marvellous Me!

A dollop of kindness
A teaspoon of love
I'm filled with emotions I couldn't dream of
A saucepan of humour
A pinch of beauty
What a super, smiling, marvellous me

My hunger for adventure
My thrill for hard work
I urge to find out things, it drives me berserk
I'm never jealous
I do not envy
I'm a clever, courageous, marvellous me

I can't wait for my future
To see what I'll be
A lawyer? Accountant? A vet?
We'll see
I'll work hard until I get there
I'll push, I guarantee
But till then, timewise, I have plenty

So I will continue to be...
My mindful, magnificent, marvellous me.

Sienna Wallen (11)

Melrose At The Ladies College, St Peter Port

This Is Me

I love my mummy, she is really nice
My hair is as dark as chocolate
My eyes are as blue as crystals
I love my older brother, he is nice
My daddy is fun but sometimes cross
Like when Harry doesn't wash his knees
Harry's dancing is so bad
Mummy is so good at art
My favourite colour is pink
I will not sink in a pool
But my daddy will
He doesn't know how to swim
He never did
We went on holiday, he nearly drowned
It was funny, but probably not for him
I am as pretty as a flower
I am as brave as a tiger.

Grace Mulholland (8)
New Row Primary School, Castledawson

Mighty Me

My name is Energetic Eliana and I'm here to say
I'm the coolest kid in the world today
I love my life, I'm as mighty as a lion
My favourite colour is blue, my eyes are too
My hair is blonde, shining like the sun
It is bright enough to blind everyone
I go to a school called New Row
Every day I wear a bow
I'm as kind as a doctor
My friends never give up on me
Always be kind, no matter what
After all, that's me!

Eliana Coleman (9)
New Row Primary School, Castledawson

Marvellous Me

I am as brave as a buffalo in a fight

R eally kind with all my might

E very day, I have an exciting time as I do when there is light

L ucky as a shamrock in spring with its delight

A nimals are as cuddly as teddies. They're like my brothers, you can play with them forever, even at

N ight

D eadly on the football pitch, kick as long as he gets the ball and hits uptight!

Daniel Gribbin (9)
New Row Primary School, Castledawson

This Is Me

S o chocolate is the best like vanilla
H e is as happy as he could be
A lways be kind and caring
N ever give up
N o one should be bad at all

J esus is important
O utside, I have a very fun time
S ay good things to people
E aster is very fun
P enguins are cute
H e was sweating in the desert!

Shann Bradley (8)
New Row Primary School, Castledawson

This Is Me

E very day my hair curls more
L oving more every day
L ike balls of fluffy kittens
I never give up
E llie is my name, thank you very much

B ig and strong like a lion
I gnoring all distractions
G rowing quick like grass
G oing on all day
E very day, I do my best
R ight here, now.

Ellie Bigger (8)

New Row Primary School, Castledawson

It's Me, Tomás

T alents are my favourite
O ctopus has eight legs
M ass is God's home
Á rtistic is a good drawing
S afe as a dog

C aring is helpful
L oving is good
E very day, I go to school
A pples I love
R eading books I like
Y ellow as the sun.

Tomas Cleary (8)
New Row Primary School, Castledawson

This Is Me

My name is Sophia,
And this is my great idea.
I'll tell you about myself,
A poem, like from a book on the bookshelf.
I have brown hair and brown eyes,
And like to think I'm very wise.
I have a brother and sister,
We all like to play Twister.
I love my daddy and mummy,
I think they are very funny.

Sophia McMullan (8)
New Row Primary School, Castledawson

This Is Senan

I am as strong as a mountain
My eyes are blue, just like you
My favourite animal is a dog
Especially mine, his name is Buddy
He goes, "Woof! Woof!"
He loves my mom
My favourite sport is football
I love it, we always win
I love basketball
I love to play with my brother
He always beats me.

Senan Lupari (8)
New Row Primary School, Castledawson

I Am Leo

I'm as happy as a kitty
I'm as cuddly as a teddy bear
My hair is as shiny as gold

I'm as loud as a dog
I can jump as high as a kangaroo
I'm as smart as a book
I'm as lucky as a shamrock

I'm as strong as an ox
I'm as sneaky as a chameleon
I am Leo G!

Leo Graham (9)
New Row Primary School, Castledawson

A Bit About Me

My name is Nicola and I have a dog and three cats,
I bet you didn't know that!
I also have a snake,
Artwork is something I love to make.
Do you know how many languages I can speak?
Two, and I think that's pretty sweet!
I am nice and kind every day,
And I have great friends and I love to play!

Nicola Szeliga (9)
New Row Primary School, Castledawson

All About Me

My hair is as brown as chocolate
And shiny like the sea
And that is a little bit about me
My favourite colour is blue like my shoes
And I am a person like you
I have a yellow pencil
And I like marshmallows
If you know me, I love eating sweets
But right now I am writing on a sheet.

Emily Young (9)
New Row Primary School, Castledawson

Thomas' Rap

I love technology
I love to bake
I love to cook
I look at the creations I cooked
I am shy and friendly and happy
Tech, tech, tech is the best
You play video games on the iPad
Phones, computer, Xbox, PS and the Switch
Tech, tech, tech is the best
You play games with tech.

Thomas Gribbin (9)
New Row Primary School, Castledawson

This Is Me

J osh is loving and kind
O ld as eight
S mart as a fox
H ome is my relaxing place

S leepy as a sloth
K ind as a bear
E xcellent as a whale
L azy as a panda
L oving, kind person
Y elled as loud as a dog.

Josh Skelly (8)
New Row Primary School, Castledawson

This Is Charlotte

C harlotte is my name
H elpful as a bee
A dventurous as I like to go for walks
R elaxing in my bed
L ovely like my mum
O utside, I have a good time
T all as a giraffe
T asty food is my favourite
E very day, I am happy.

Charlotte Bothwell (8)
New Row Primary School, Castledawson

This Is Me

R afferty is my name

A ctive as I play Camogie

F unny as a puppy

F unny as I like to make people laugh

E xcited as a kid at Christmas

R elax with my music

T an skin shines and my brown hair

Y ou can't beat me, I am the best.

Rafferty Hassan (9)
New Row Primary School, Castledawson

This Is Me

I am as fast as a cheetah
I am as cold as an iceberg
I am as brave as a lion
I am as skinny as Flat Stanley
I am as long as a crane
I am as hairy as a bear
I am as fancy as a millionaire
I am as big as the galaxy
I am as nice as a gentleman!

Phelim Kealey (8)

New Row Primary School, Castledawson

This Is Me

I am as sneaky as a racoon
I'm always happy to learn new things
I'm very kind
I've got a big brain that's always growing
I'm as fast as Usain Bolt
I'm as funny as a clown
My favourite food is pizza
I am as brave as a lion.

Noah Gribbin (9)
New Row Primary School, Castledawson

I'm Me Because I'm Me

My eyes are as blue as the ocean
And as sparkly as the moon

My drawings are good
When I am in the mood

I can run really fast
'Cause I never come last

My kittens are as fluffy as mittens
But I would prefer a puffy puppy.

Juliette Konkiewicz (8)
New Row Primary School, Castledawson

Sean's Song

I love the Switch
But I hate a witch
I am a ship
Like the Titanic
But I'll never give up
Even if I sink
But wait
It's not the end
The time is bending
But we've wasted
All of our time
So we're done!

Sean Lavery (8)

New Row Primary School, Castledawson

I Am Me

I am as brave as a baboon
I'm as silly as sweets
My hair is as dark as night
I am as sharp as a porcupine
I am swimming like a fish
I am as sneaky as a rat
I'm cold like an ice cream
I am as sporty as a PE teacher.

Michael McLarnon (8)
New Row Primary School, Castledawson

Facts About Me, Senan Hughes

I am as strong and brave as a buffalo
I am as fast as a rocket going up to space
I am a mighty midfielder in soccer and Gaelic
I can jump as high as a kangaroo
I am as smart as a super teacher
I am as funny as a clown at a circus.

Senan Hughes (8)
New Row Primary School, Castledawson

I Am Chloe

Above me are clouds as soft as pillows
Below me is grass as spiky as a pinprick
Beside me is my family
Around me is the universe
At school, I have my friends
At home, I feel nice and cosy
I am proud to say... I am Chloe!

Chloe Doherty (8)
New Row Primary School, Castledawson

Marvellous Me

D aire is a great singer

A nd he is funny and he makes a lot of money

I am good at art, sharing and caring

R eally kind and has a big mind

E nthusiastic and he is friendly and he is handsome.

Daire McErlean (8)

New Row Primary School, Castledawson

This Is Saoirse

My skin is as pale as the colour whitish peach
My hair is as orange as a carrot
My eyes are as green as grass
My family is as sweet as sugar
I love my life, I love my friends and family
And that's that.

Saoirse Martin (9)
New Row Primary School, Castledawson

Clever Caolan

C hristmas is cool like ice
A nd autumn is too
O ver the moon, I go
L eaving space again
A ctivities, I like to play football
N ever trust November.

Caolan Fitzsimons (9)
New Row Primary School, Castledawson

Conan

C onan is my name
O n Halloween, I get sweets
N ever give up on gaming
A dventurous, I like to explore outside
N avy uniform is what I wear to school.

Conan Lagan (8)
New Row Primary School, Castledawson

Cool Cathal

When I look up at the sky
The sky looks down at me
I like myself
I like people
I like my family
I like my sisters
My mummy and daddy
I am as fast as a cheetah.

Cathal Gallagher (8)
New Row Primary School, Castledawson

This Is Me

E abha is my name
A ttractive as candy
B eautiful like my mum
H ealthy as I like to eat apples
A lways being helpful and never ungrateful.

Eabha Totten (8)

New Row Primary School, Castledawson

This Is My Poem

L ovely
O ptimistic
V ery inviting
E xcited
L ove dogs
Y ou are happy and kind

I am an eagle, smart and strong.

Kathryn McLaughlin (8)

New Row Primary School, Castledawson

Fantastic Elliot

I am as fast as a cheetah
I am as brave as a tiger
I am as sneaky as a squirrel
My eyes are blue
I can jump as high as a kangaroo
I am as tall as a giraffe.

Elliot Smyth (8)
New Row Primary School, Castledawson

This Is Carol

C aring as a teacher
A rtistic as art
R iddletastic as a riddle
O rdinary as a person
L ovely as I'm pretty.

Carol Ferris (9)

New Row Primary School, Castledawson

This Is Me Recipe

Three teaspoons of funniness
100 grams of happiness
A pinch of horse-filled bedroom
A gallon of horse craziness
A pound of friends and friendliness
Mix it all around with a shake of purple shavings
Add a tablespoon of blanket-covered book reading
And a kilogram of kindness as you whisk it
all together
Season to taste with speckles of sportiness
And decorate with mellow marshmallow-roasting
camping trips
Finally, serve with a slice of animal-loving
chocolate cake
With melt in the middle chocolate sauce,
chocolate sprinkles
A chocolate flake, and a little bit more chocolate...

Megan Pyke (10)
Oystermouth Primary School, Mumbles

This Is Me

M axwell and Ioan are my friends

A rt is the best hobby

R emus Lupin is my favourite Harry Potter character

I love dogs, they are so cute

N uggets and chips

E loise is my sister's name

B ig brainer

I am as bright as the sun

O ctopi are my favourite animals

L azy like a sloth

O ranges are delicious

G ob is where I put food

I dislike coffee, it is too bitter

S prite is the most amazing beverage

T alented at art!

Charlie
Oystermouth Primary School, Mumbles

Dream Day

Coco-Pops with salted caramel ice cream with
wafers on top
Sunny, sparkling sun shining across the sea
I'm with Esterban and Monty and my dogs,
Pickle and Zac
Playing tennis on clouds in the sky, bouncing onto
one another
And sliding down a rainbow with my gramps in
our pyjamas
I spotted thirty different types of beds
I hear the sound of the waves crashing against the
rocks at the beach
At night, I sleep in a grand palace in the grand
bedroom with the smell of waffles being
cooked downstairs.

Indi Belton (10)
Oystermouth Primary School, Mumbles

This Is What I Am!

M y name is Meghan

E nergy is something I have most of

G reen is the colour of my eyes and it is my fave colour

H appy is what I like being

A mint ice cream always cheers me up when I am sad

N utella is what I eat most of

C hameleons are my favourite animal

L ove is what my family gives me

I am most definitely book crazy

F or breakfast I love pancakes

T ime for bed is the worst part of the day!

Meghan Clift (10)

Oystermouth Primary School, Mumbles

Dream Day

American pancakes with the world's biggest GG's
Ferrero ice cream, sprinkled with M&Ms
Snow sparkling in the cold garden
I'm with Oti Mabuse and my dog, Star and sitting
on a cold garden bench
I am swimming across the world's biggest pool and
dancing on a rooftop building doing the samba
Nine pieces of sushi filled with ice cream and
chocolate mooncakes
I can hear drums in the distance of metropolis
marshmallow
Sleeping on a bed full of candyfloss.

Samuel Harris (9)
Oystermouth Primary School, Mumbles

Dream Day

For breakfast, I'm having pancakes with brownies
and chocolate sauce and mint choc chip ice cream
and hot chocolate
The weather is cloudy, crazy and bright
I'm with my fluffy dogs and my friends and my
flying monkey
I went in VR and played Roblox with my friends
in Greek
Eleven of each chocolate in the universe amongst
me and my friends
The sound of the warm ocean crashing against the
rocky wall
At night, I sleep in the comfiest bed in the world.

Ned Calder (9)
Oystermouth Primary School, Mumbles

Dream Day

Chocolate sauce-covered hot sugar doughnuts
with bright colourful sprinkles
Snow slowly settles and soothing suburban houses
I'm with a sparkly Siberian howling husky
Snowboarding down a slippy, slidey, snowy slope
with my fastest, funniest friends
Twelve hoarding huskies with horrendous hugs,
with twelve covering cute faces
A sound of falling flakes, freezing when they
touch your tongue
I slept on the soft, smooth snow, cuddling up
to a husky.

Alfred Ronnie Williams (9)
Oystermouth Primary School, Mumbles

Dream Day

Mint ice cream and pancakes with hot chocolate
It rains many marvellous marshmallows, colours of
the rainbow
A glorious day to share with my mischievous
brother and all my friends
Standing on the acting stage directed by
William Shakespeare
Walking along the Amalfi coast, five little dogs
tagging along beside me
I hear the *woof!* of my puppies and the sway
of the sea.
Sleeping soundly on a cloud of candyfloss, thinking
of my dream day...

Daisy Spatuzzi (9)
Oystermouth Primary School, Mumbles

Dream Day

Four scoops of raspberry ripple, five pancakes
and macarons
Sunny seas shining across the seven seas
It's me, my family and friends spending this day
with me
Playing football with my friends on the Scarlet Bay
Four magical rainbow dolphins dancing in the sea
The crashing waves on the bay, children laughing,
saying, "It's such a great day!"
Sleeping in the sea, whales are surrounding me
and rainbow dolphins singing a melody.

Ellen Curley (9)
Oystermouth Primary School, Mumbles

Dream Day

Twenty stacks of chocolate and banana pancakes
with ten plates of every flavour cake
The sparkling sun shining on the stunning city
It's me and my goofy bestie
Going to Paris and stuffing my face with baguette
Fourteen baguettes safely in my roaring stomach
French bands playing their happy, joyful music
At night, I sleep in a fancy French hotel in silky
sheets of sparkly silver, dreaming of dancing pigs
in space, wearing neon pink jumpsuits.

Erin Porter (10)
Oystermouth Primary School, Mumbles

Dream Day

Bogey ice cream with eye bogey sprinkles and a
side of snot
Eye bursting, floor-breaking bellowing thunder
I'm with amazing, courageous Tom Holland
I am swimming in the shark-infested ocean with a
sea-blue surfboard
The seven dwarves are sprinting around me in a
circle singing their spectacular song
The melody of the sea dancing around me
At night, I sleep by the warm fire on the soft sand,
staring at the spectacular sunset.

Eryn Harwood (9)
Oystermouth Primary School, Mumbles

Dream Day

Crispy, creamy pancakes and chocolate ice cream
The sparkly sun glistens in the sky
It's me, family and friends enjoying my dream day
Playing football on the sunny Australian beach
along with Ronaldo
Twelve Harry Potter actors crowding me with
autographs in a jungle
The sound of the sea crashing against the
huge rocks
At night, I sleep in a gorgeous Australian beach
hut listening to the crashing waves.

Maia Hayward (10)
Oystermouth Primary School, Mumbles

Dream Day

Biscoff pancakes with salted caramel ice cream
Snowy snowman sparkles on my garden grass
I'm with my whole family, cousins and my
dog, Bella
I am paddle-boarding in the middle of Antarctica
With dolphins and penguins
I'm playing fetch with eleven white and brown
border collies in Antarctica
I hear snow foxes playing with their cubs
At night, I sleep on a colourful cloud with my
dog, Bella.

Elsie Brain (9)
Oystermouth Primary School, Mumbles

My Dream Day

Warm chocolate brownies and vanilla ice cream
A wonderfully warm day spitting with marvellous melted chocolate
Crowded with all my fabulous friends
Playing a huge game of hide-and-seek up in the mountains
I caught ten delicious drops of chocolate falling from the sky
A whole flock of beautiful robins came tweeting past me
I stayed up until the early hours of the morning and I fell asleep gazing at the stars.

Aisha Keogh (10)
Oystermouth Primary School, Mumbles

Dream Day

French toast with honey
The stormy snow was like an ice age
I'm with my ginormous dog
My mum and dad come along
We made a shed with logs

I swam with the Olympic team
I did surfing in the deep waters of Hawaii
I drove to Legoland and met the Lego team

I ate feijoada for dinner
I put off the heating
I put my warm pyjamas on
I slept in the most expensive house.

Pietro Da Silva (9)
Oystermouth Primary School, Mumbles

Dream Day

Chocolate ice cream and pancakes with
chocolate sauce
Windy, whooshy wind travels across the world
It's my dog, Gibbsy, gathering around the crowd
I landed across the football pitch to play
for England
I have doughnuts to celebrate, it's my dream day
I found my favourite soundtrack, the Coffin Dance
At night, I sleep on a king-size bed, well, I'm
making the most of my dream day.

Joshua Alkarnaz (9)
Oystermouth Primary School, Mumbles

Dream Day

French toast with cinnamon and honey
The sun was shimmering down on the hot sand
In the dangerous deadly crashing plane, my dad
was there for me
The chess characters were so big, you needed a
plane to carry them across
the board
Ten deadly soldiers retreated across the battlefield
There was a loud screaming siren in the air
I was sleeping in an untidy bed in an allied base
in Britain.

Dylan Ravitz (9)
Oystermouth Primary School, Mumbles

This Is Me

For this you will need:
One gram of kindness
A spoon of sweetness
A slice of pizza
A cup of sugar
And the secret ingredient, a pinch of laughter

After that:
Mix them altogether
Then scoop onto a baking tray
Leave in the oven for fifteen minutes
Take out of the oven and place onto a plate
Let cool for five minutes
Add a dollop of mint choc chip ice cream
And you have me!

Seren James (10)
Oystermouth Primary School, Mumbles

This Is Me

For this you will need:
A cup of kindness
A sprinkle of joy
A dash of laughter too
A splash of care
A room full of art supplies

You will need to:
Pour your cup of kindness into a bowl
Next, add your splash of care
And just for taste, a sprinkle of joy
After that, a dash of laughter
And finally, a room full of art supplies
Bake in the oven for fifteen minutes, until
fully baked
Then, you have finished.

Olivia Kenna (11)
Oystermouth Primary School, Mumbles

Dream Day

Ten giant chocolate-covered pancakes and two
massive bottles of lemonade
The stunning sun shining through the clouds
I'm with family on a tropical beach
Covered in paint and rolling on a giant canvas
Seven ginger cats cuddled around me
A playlist of all my favourite songs playing on a
massive speaker
At night, I fall asleep on the beach in a rainbow
hammock watching the sun set.

Emily-Rose Walker (9)
Oystermouth Primary School, Mumbles

Dream Day

Nutella covered pancakes with chocolate
ice cream
Snowy cold weather in a cosy calm cottage
It's me with my family, friends and pets
Ziplining in space while waving to green,
gross aliens
Nine sparkly, fresh Lamborghinis waiting to
be driven
I hear the snow hitting the roof of the cottage
I'm in the world's comfiest bed, gazing at the stars.

Elin Koscian (10)
Oystermouth Primary School, Mumbles

Dream Day

Seventeen scoops of lemon sorbet and a waffle
with macarons
Snowy snow squirrels spiral to the ground
I'm with Miss Whittington, my TA
Swimming in the Bermuda Triangle, investigating
the lost
Twelve cases unsolved
'Stressed Out' by Twenty-One Pilots playing in
my ear
I'm sleeping in a hammock listening to the
waves crashing against the rocks.

Elijah Coughan (9)
Oystermouth Primary School, Mumbles

Dream Day

Ice cream, chocolate cake, jelly and pancakes
The sun shines on the sea and sparkled on
the grass
I'm here with my flying dog, Molly
Playing football with all my friends on the moon
with Messi
Seven chocolate cookies with chocolate sauce
A dragon roaring like a baby screeching
Sleeping on the bottom of the ocean in a dark
cave with sharks circling around.

Grayson Thomas (9)
Oystermouth Primary School, Mumbles

Dream Day

Chocolate pancakes with vanilla ice cream
Sparkling snow falling from the sky
I'm with my family, friends and Lamby
Camping at Mount Everest with a yeti groaning at
the bottom
Twelve pieces of mochi followed by fresh,
fabulous sushi
A hoot of an owl as I walk through the forest
Sleeping in the cosiest bed in a treehouse in the
dark Russian forest.

Ted Thomas (9)
Oystermouth Primary School, Mumbles

Dream Day

Krave for breakfast, it's my favourite
Raining rats are falling down
I'm with my best bud, Ben
We are in a football centre playing for Liverpool
My number is ten and Ben's is eleven
We could hear the fans chanting, "You'll never
walk alone!" It was so loud
When I was on the bench at full-time, I
was sleeping.

Louie Beck (9)
Oystermouth Primary School, Mumbles

Dream Day

Chocolate pancakes with chocolate ice cream
and sprinkles
The sparkling sun shining in the sky
It's me and my family and my dog
Surfing in the wild west sea with my best friend,
Elin, in Hawaii
Eight delicious cupcakes shared with my family
The wild waves crashing against the rocks
I am sleeping in a cosy, warm cottage.

Caitlin Vaughan (9)
Oystermouth Primary School, Mumbles

This Is Me

I am amazing at swimming like a shark
I am a superstar swimmer
I dive in the sea like a miraculous dolphin
I run to the sea as soon as it hits 3:00
I go into the deep end with no fear
I like platypuses, they're my favourite animal
I am as accurate as a lionfish
I love dipping in the sea on a hot summer's day.

Maxwell Fuller (10)
Oystermouth Primary School, Mumbles

This Is Me

T he grass is greener under me as
H appy as can be
I love the sea as cold as can be and
S ummer is the time for me

I 'm a chocolate lover and in the
S ummer I'm a water rocker

M eghan Trainer is my favourite singer and an
E lephant is all I hear.

Ella Jardine
Oystermouth Primary School, Mumbles

Dream Day

A full English breakfast
Rampages of runny rain
I'm with my auntie because she lets me go
on nice trips
I would like to go on the Hex: The Legend of the
Towers at Alton Towers
Twenty-eight seats on a roller coaster ride
Spooky music trying to scare people
I like Cialla's spare bed in her spare room.

Cai Clement (10)
Oystermouth Primary School, Mumbles

Dream Day

Ice cream pancakes with fresh juice
Sun shines in the small sea
All my magnificent friends come along
We bike to the moon on a ramp
We play football up here
We spend seven hours up at night having fun
I can hear the sound of the crashing sea
My friends and I sleep up in the treehouse with 100 floors.

Bodhi Maddern Nixon (10)
Oystermouth Primary School, Mumbles

This Is Me

80lbs of football with a light stir
2lbs of Chelsea
4lbs of defender
Five tons of football boots with shin pads
A pinch of rugby
A splash of any other sport
Three tons of maths with another little splash
Zero tons of science with minus a pinch
Mix it with chicken and fries
And a splash of chocolate milk
And my very favourite...
Is me.

Louis Franklin (11)
Oystermouth Primary School, Mumbles

Dream Day

Banana and strawberry with chocolate ice cream
Shiny sun on sparkling sea
It's me, Mum and Dad hear
Minecraft is magical, mystical and marvellous
Fourteen minutes of marvellous mayhem
I hear ACDC 'Back in Black'
I'm sleeping on a camping ground
We can hear a beast out there.

Ben Smith (9)
Oystermouth Primary School, Mumbles

My Dream

My dream is to become an artist
I have my own technique
Which is unique
A swish and a sway with a brush
The colour is ever so lush
My picture is full of colour
There is nothing to cover
Ready to be admired
Free to inspire
My favourite colours
Pink, yellow and blue
Art is one of my favourite things to do.

Anjali Munnangi (10)

Oystermouth Primary School, Mumbles

Dream Day

Pancakes with milk and orange fruit
The sunny sparkly sea
It's my dream day of getting my dog called Chase
I like cycling on the cycling path
Six scrumptious chocolate cakes with cream
Birds singing a beat
Go to a very nice hotel where the sun sets over
the sea.

Harri Davies (9)
Oystermouth Primary School, Mumbles

Dream Day

Seventeen sweets and ice cream
Sun shining through the sparkling window
I'm with Winnie the Pooh and Thumper
I would draw on top of a mountain
Two massive pieces of chocolate
I can hear the dinner bell
I sleep on a bouncy castle made of chocolate.

Bethan Lewis (9)
Oystermouth Primary School, Mumbles

The Party

In the start, we made slime
And I thought I was out of time
Then we played a nice tune
We played till the full moon

After that, we ate food
Then I was in a good mood
I was running around like a monkey
I was dancing, feeling funky

We went to play chess
I felt like the best.

Ioan Jones (11)
Oystermouth Primary School, Mumbles

This Is Me

If I stand in a crowd, I think you see me
I am also quite a tennis player, challenge me if
you dare
I am easily distracted so I take a century to finish
my work
My spirit animal is a bunny because of my big
bunny teeth
And if go on a walk I am always clumsy
This is me!

James Dumpleton
Oystermouth Primary School, Mumbles

This Is Me

T he cricket field is my favourite place
H elpful
I love sport
S cience is my future

I maginative
S uper crazy over lemurs

M assive gamer
E quation master.

Elliott
Oystermouth Primary School, Mumbles

This Is Me

T errific at gaming
H uge duck fan
I ncredibly funny
S ongs I love

I s great at technology
S uper soft pet cat, Abby

M inecraft mad
E xcellent at maths.

Aeron Wilson Whitcombe

Oystermouth Primary School, Mumbles

Dream Day

Waffle with ice cream and Nutella
Lovely soft snowy snow
I am with sweetie dogs, Bax and Stan
Playing with my lovely dogs
Playing with six cute dogs
Massive snow crashing down
At the best little cottage.

Orla Richards (9)
Oystermouth Primary School, Mumbles

This Is Me

T alented footballer
H ates math
I ncredibly chatty
S uper brave

I love baking
S ometimes too crazy

M ad dog, Bella
E arly riser.

Nell Brain
Oystermouth Primary School, Mumbles

This Is Me

I have a hamster as white as snow
I like going in the sea when it is cold
I like playing football in the rain
Once the cows are running away
My clothes are as green as a frog
I like playing netball under the sun
This is me.

Sofia Sewell Hunter (10)
Oystermouth Primary School, Mumbles

If I Were An Animal

If I were an animal, I would be a frog
All day I can sit under a log
Eating flies all night long
Whilst the birds are chirping a song
As the church bells are going *ding-dong!*
All the children will be hopping along.

Lyla Jonsson (11)
Oystermouth Primary School, Mumbles

Staffy

S uper at maths
T alks a lot
A good friend
F avourite sport is football
F avourite subject is maths
Y ellow and black are my favourite colours.

Ethan (10)

Oystermouth Primary School, Mumbles

This Is Me

I am as bright as a star
My eyes are green emeralds
Monkeys are my favourite
Because they are cheeky and joyful
Singing is my speciality
I am a book lover
And a kind cookie
This is me.

Olivia B
Oystermouth Primary School, Mumbles

Dream Day

Christmas pudding
Sparkly snow
With Mummy
I would fly in a train to space
Seven cheesy pizzas
Thomas theme tune plays
I sleep in a bouncy castle.

Lex Morgan (9)
Oystermouth Primary School, Mumbles

About Me

I am a llama lover
Netball player
Food eater
Early riser
Curry lover
I have three sisters
I love raspberries
And I'm a good friend!

Bella Morgan (11)
Oystermouth Primary School, Mumbles

I Am Me

I am me
I am extraordinary
I am like a bird flying high in the sky
My eyes sparkle like on the darkest nights
My voice sings like a songbird in its nest
My hair is as black as the night
My skin shines like a goddess on the River Nile
I am me.

Ruth Kaputa (11)
Pimlico Academy, Westminster

This Is Me

My hair is brown like a chocolate bar
I like my hair because it is soft like a cloth
My hair is as short as my bottle
My hair is fun to play with on a long journey
When I wash my hair, I don't need to dry it because
it dries really fast
My eyebrows are as bushy as a bush
My eyebrows are the colour of a tree trunk
My eyebrows are a bit thick and chunky like
a monkey
My eyebrows are long and elegant
I love my eyebrows, if I scratch them they won't
get ruined.

Eriona Ahmeti
Richmond Avenue Primary School, Shoeburyness

This Is Me And My Legs

My legs are sadly bruised quite a lot
They have a lot of hair
My legs are nearly as long as an elephant's trunk
My legs are as tall as a skyscraper
They are also nearly as light as a lighthouse light
I love my legs because they are almost always
covered in bruises
Bruises help me remember good and bad times
Altogether, they are quite amazing
I really do approve of them.

Reuben Mayne (8)
Richmond Avenue Primary School, Shoeburyness

My Great Hair

My hair is as soft as a pillow,
So soft and prickly, wow
I like my hair because it is soft like a cloth
My hair is brown and kind of gold
My hair is brown like chocolate
My hair is as thin as silk and as tight as a pie
I love my hair because it is soft, brown and gold
I love my hair because it is very fun to play with
And very soggy in water.

Eliot Bodacz (7)

Richmond Avenue Primary School, Shoeburyness

The Best Part Of Me

I like my hair, my long brown hair
When I get nits, it really does itch
I bet I'm just like Stitch
My brown hair is long and wavy
I really think it goes with navy
When you see me, you'll think I'm a bear
Because this hair really does scare!

Evie Shepherd (7)
Richmond Avenue Primary School, Shoeburyness

The Best Part Of Me

The best part of me is my hair
My hair is golden and glossy like a diamond
My hair is gold like the sun
My hair is sparkly if you look closely
If you look closer, you can see brown
My hair is wavy like the wind
In the shower, it turns dark brown.

Millie (7)
Richmond Avenue Primary School, Shoeburyness

This Is Me

My hair is brown
My hair goes down
My hair is soft
My hair flows in the loft
My hair is as brown as chocolate
My hair goes in my yoghurt
My hair is as soft as a pillow
My hair gets stuck in marshmallow
My hair is as short as a ruler.

Matilda Rutt (7)
Richmond Avenue Primary School, Shoeburyness

The Best Part Of Me

My hair is cute like a bunny in a suit
It's wavy and I think I'm going to dye it navy
It's truly amazing and the clouds
Are all gazing at my wonderful hair
It flops like a mop
It floats like bubbles but it causes no trouble.

Rosemary Palmer (8)
Richmond Avenue Primary School, Shoeburyness

My Nice Poem

My hair is blonde
My hair is long
My hair is straight
My hair is as smooth as a sloth
My hair is growing a fringe
My hair is as pretty as a pink petal
My hair is as cool as a koala
My hair is as fluffy as a cute puppy.

Amy Stoner (8)
Richmond Avenue Primary School, Shoeburyness

The Best Part Of Me

My hair is as brown as a clown
It's as smooth as a groove
It's as shiny as the Pacific Ocean
I have no devotion
My hair is as short as a baby book
It's dark, that's true, it makes me go, "Moo!"

Isla Divall (7)

Richmond Avenue Primary School, Shoeburyness

All About Me

I love me
I like my hair
My hair is soft
I like my eyes
My eyes are shiny
I like my teeth
My teeth are white
I like my wrist
My wrist is like a handle
I like my feet
My feet help me walk.

Scarlett Wood (7)

Richmond Avenue Primary School, Shoeburyness

The Best Of Me

My hair is short
It is brown like a bear
I like my hair because I like that it is like a big field
My hair is as smooth as a table
I love my hair because it's different to
everyone else's.

Austin Higgins (7)
Richmond Avenue Primary School, Shoeburyness

The Best Part Of Me

My hair is cute like a Fruit Loop.
It is very wavy and I might dye it navy.
Once I felt it my face looked relaxed,
because it is so soft.
My friends love me because of my hair.
And I love them.

Jessica Jackson (7)
Richmond Avenue Primary School, Shoeburyness

This Is Me

My mouth is as big as a giraffe's mouth
My mouth is big outside and inside
My mouth is red inside

I like my teeth, they are straight
I like my lips because they are really straight.

Liberty Hall (7)
Richmond Avenue Primary School, Shoeburyness

The Best Part Of Me

I like my best-at-running feet
They're peach like the rest of my body
I like my smelly feet
I couldn't swing on the swings without them
They're not colourful like a rainbow.

Maisie Giles (7)
Richmond Avenue Primary School, Shoeburyness

The Best Part Of Me

The best part of me is my ears, my floppy ears
Whenever you bend them, they always flop back
The peach colour comes from my family
I like my ears because they help me listen to songs.

Thomas Bannister (7)
Richmond Avenue Primary School, Shoeburyness

This Is Me

My hair is as brown as a tree branch
It is really smooth
It has golden ends
The ends are as golden as a golden coin
It is as smooth as paper
My hair is as long as a ruler.

Evie Saville (7)
Richmond Avenue Primary School, Shoeburyness

The Best Part Of Me

The best part of me is my legs
They are long like a cheetah
My legs are good to me
Because they help me to run
My legs are fun to me
Because I want to be able to swim.

Seth Brown (7)
Richmond Avenue Primary School, Shoeburyness

The Best Part Of Me

The best part of me is my head
And my beautiful face
Because it hides a big brain
That helps with my math and English
I wouldn't be able to learn.

Reuben Clark (7)
Richmond Avenue Primary School, Shoeburyness

My Hair

I like my hair because it is long
My hair is golden
I like my hair because it is curly
My hair is long
It is brown a little bit.

Matilda White (7)
Richmond Avenue Primary School, Shoeburyness

The Best Part Of Me

I love my strong, muscly legs
They help me jump on the trampoline
I love my legs
Because they help me run fast like a cheetah.

Lily Dickenson (7)
Richmond Avenue Primary School, Shoeburyness

The Best Part Of Me

The best part of me is my eyes
They help me see the skies
The best part of me is my eyes
They are as blue as Blu-Tak.

Olivia Tofts (7)
Richmond Avenue Primary School, Shoeburyness

This Is Me

My legs are hairy
My legs are very, very bruised
I have lots of scratches
They are the strongest part of my body.

Angus Gavin (8)
Richmond Avenue Primary School, Shoeburyness

The Best Part Of Me

The best part of me is my hair
Because it is long and blonde
Like a soft blonde banana
It is crazy like Maisie.

Gabrielle Ellis (7)
Richmond Avenue Primary School, Shoeburyness

The Best Part Of Me

I like my eyes
Because I can see with them
I watch where I am going
My eyes are as green as the grass.

Mia Takacs (7)
Richmond Avenue Primary School, Shoeburyness

The Best Part Of Me

I love my eyes
Because they are brown like chocolate
I love my eyes
Because they sparkle like a star.

Sebastian Quayle (7)
Richmond Avenue Primary School, Shoeburyness

This Is Me

My hands are red
My hands are smooth and soft
I love my hands
Because they let me play Xbox.

Zakk Edwards (8)
Richmond Avenue Primary School, Shoeburyness

My Eyes Help Me

My eyes help me to see
My eyes are brown
They are also white
My eyes are big.

Sidney Tuffin (7)
Richmond Avenue Primary School, Shoeburyness

Jack

My arm can twist like a handle
I can stretch my arm
It is as hairy as a monkey.

Jack Conner (7)
Richmond Avenue Primary School, Shoeburyness

This Is Me

My hand is soft
I feel stuff with my helpful hand
I like to clap fast and loud.

Lucas Hughes (7)

Richmond Avenue Primary School, Shoeburyness

The Best Part Of Me

The best part of me is my toes
Because they are curly
Like sausages.

Liam Williams (7)
Richmond Avenue Primary School, Shoeburyness

My Legs

My legs are skinny
I can do front flips
I can do side flips.

Riley Caron (7)
Richmond Avenue Primary School, Shoeburyness

The Best Part Of Me

I like my hair
It is fluffy like a pillow
My hair is soft.

Riley-Rae Dadds (7)

Richmond Avenue Primary School, Shoeburyness

The Best Part Of Me

My hair is brown
It is wavy
It is like the sea.

Arianna Causova (7)
Richmond Avenue Primary School, Shoeburyness

Teddy Goes To Space!

One day, the Earth erupted!
You would have needed to stay in your houses
But me and Teddy escaped
We put on our spacesuits
And a fast booster
Then we set off
First, we went to the shiny moon
We met some mysterious aliens
Their skin was as green as grass
Suddenly, we found a football
It looked like Mars
Teddy ran to pick it up
Even though it was on fire.

David Gabor (8)
The St Teresa Catholic Primary School, Dagenham

My Shy Life

My name is Shreya
I am really really shy and quiet
I am as shy as a mouse
I am as shy as a rat
I think to myself
Can I come out of the shell I am stuck in?

Whenever I need to stand in front of the call
I use my quiet voice
But whenever I am with my family or friends
I use my biggest voice ever
My friends and family keep saying
"Shreya, why don't you use this big voice
in school?"
I sit there and think, *why don't I?*

The next day I had to read a poem at the front
of the class
I absolutely felt embarrassed
Because everyone kept on saying

"Shout! Shout! Shout!"
I stood there and thought, *why don't I?*

Shreya Solan (8)
The St Teresa Catholic Primary School, Dagenham

This Is Me!

I like Minecraft
As well as pizza, like everyone

I love learning about history
And playing TTRS on my tablet

I am sometimes independent
I try to do my best, but then I rest

I run and have fun
But then sometimes I play football

I'm as fast as lightning
I run faster than my friend, soaring through the
wind

I play on my tablet for hours
Forgetting to do my homework!

I live in the east, the opposite of west
In a normal house, on a normal street

I can do a wheelie on a scooter
And I can ride as fast as a cheetah on a bike

This is a poem about me
Not anyone else.

Johann Joseph (8)
The St Teresa Catholic Primary School, Dagenham

My Life Journey!

I am a dreamer
When I read... I travel to exotic places
When I write... the words are colours
When I swim... I see dolphins and fishes around me
When I dance... the studio is full of butterflies
When I help people... I see the love of God
When I fall... I see resilience and I start again
Who am I?

Answer: I am an ordinary girl in a wonderful world!

Sofia Takacs (8)
The St Teresa Catholic Primary School, Dagenham

All About Me

I am smart and gentle
I am helpful too
I feel joyful to use a sketch pad
I am a rapper, a footballer
With lightning bolt feet
I am fast like a cheetah and a Roblox player
My favourite heroes are PJ Masks and
Miraculous too
My favourite country is France
I love to read and play
I am an animal lover
I am sporty, chatty and a PS4 player.

Francis Nnaike (9)
The St Teresa Catholic Primary School, Dagenham

Myself

I am as gentle as a swan landing on a pond
I am a dog barking at a tree
I am an animal lover
Cats and dogs are my favourites
I am an energetic tiger running through the jungle
I am helpful like a buzzing bee collecting honey
My hair is brown like a wooden branch
I'm as cheeky as a monkey
When I am all these things I feel like myself.

Sarah Lalu (8)
The St Teresa Catholic Primary School, Dagenham

My Six Favourite Things

M y Nintendo Switch is my favourite gadget

A plate of chicken nuggets is my favourite food

R ice is my favourite carbohydrate

C reamy toffees are my favourite sweets

U sing paper to make comics is my favourite thing to do when I'm bored

S inking my head in the bucket is my favourite thing to do in the bath.

Marcus Icaro (8)
The St Teresa Catholic Primary School, Dagenham

I Want A Kitten

I want a kitten
As cute as I love it
I hope they're fluffy
Just like a puppy

I want a kitten
Not a pet chicken
As talented as a star
I want it to fill up my heart

I want a kitten
Not get bitten
I don't want a bat
Not even get scratched.

Rochelle Itonga (8)
The St Teresa Catholic Primary School, Dagenham

What I Like Doing

I like colouring
I like running
I am fun
When I am sad
I like hugging my teddy
I like pandas and puppies
I am happy, sometimes sad
I would like a puppy in the future
I like riding my bike
I like reading books
I like drawing.

Isla Robertson (8)

The St Teresa Catholic Primary School, Dagenham

This Is All About Me

I am funny also kind at the same time
I am patient with people
I am passionate and smart
If someone is lonely I come to them
When someone is hurt I talk to them
I have fun playing with lots of different people
If someone falls over I help them.

Andreja Andreja (8)
The St Teresa Catholic Primary School, Dagenham

Guess Who

A kennings poem

I am a...
Lego builder
Dog lover
Football player
Fortnite gamer
Maccy D's muncher
Friend maker
Bike rider
Lazy sleeper
Zoo visitor
Good swimmer
Pokémon collector

Yes, it's me, Tommy!

Tommy Grote
The St Teresa Catholic Primary School, Dagenham

This Is Me

S ome people say that I'm scary
N obody believes me when I say I'm friendly
A ll I want is a friend
K nowing that I'm deadly
E very time I'm sleepy.

Youjin Son (8)

The St Teresa Catholic Primary School, Dagenham

Anger And Kindness Can Match

With the spitfire temper that dominates me
The fireworks that curse my anger
The model trains
That took me and my grandad a lot of work
With my sporty attitude
And the gamer vibes that lay high in my heart
My fireworks of anger
Will make me a person you fear.
But a lot of times, I can be happy, kind
Everything a friend needs.
I find it hard to keep my mad, sad emotions in me
But with my family and friends backing me up
I want those fireworks not to surface
Though it's probably impossible.
But my football, train, Xbox
And car activities distract me.
Fireworks dominate me.
I hate change but I try to act normal.
This is me.

Dan Bull (10)
The Welbourn CE Primary School, Welbourn

Camping Is My Hobby!

Tea time...
Set the fire, cook some burgers
Open a packet of marshmallows
Then start to cook
Stay up late, play cards and sit by the fire
Jump in your bed, listen to the birds and wind

Morning...
The sun's bright and the sky is blue
Make your breakfast, watch the view
Brush your teeth, wash up
Walk your dog for an hour
Come back

Dinner time...
Make sandwiches and crisps
Start to munch
It's nearly time to go
Get in the car, drive to the beach
Splash and play
Time to go

Pack the tent and get ready for the long journey ahead!

Camping is my hobby!

George K (9)
The Welbourn CE Primary School, Welbourn

This Is Me

My body shakes
I stretch my arms out
Wide as they can be
I look down nervously
Everyone has their eyes on me
Sweat tingles down my blushing cheeks
I quickly brush it off my face
Standing on the gymnastics beam
I don't want to fail
It would be a total waste.

Fingers rattle
Biting my bleeding lip
I hesitate.
I hold my tear-stained head high
A sickening lump is trapped
Inside the depths of my throat
A nervous wreck
About to fall
About to give up
I find myself jumping
Desperate,

I land wobbly on two feet.
I've learned to never give up.

Lottie Bull (10)
The Welbourn CE Primary School, Welbourn

My Favourites

Foxes are noble creatures
Golden, stealthy, wise
Blue is the colour
Of the beautiful seas and skies

Football is the greatest sport
And Spurs are the best team
Art is the best
With its oranges, purples and greens

Curry is amazing
With all kinds of spice
All my friends and family
Are all very nice

Poppies are awesome
With crimson-coloured petals
Winter is cool and fun
When the snow settles

Comics are nice to read
Pow! Crash! Bash! Boom!

Pepsi Max cherry
I'm going to have some soon!

Finlay G (9)

The Welbourn CE Primary School, Welbourn

Recipe For Me!

100 pounds of craziness
A box full of McDonald's
Three pinches of laziness

Get a spoon and stir for three minutes

A Domino's pizza
And a bottle of Coca-Cola
To make the perfect meal

Five teaspoons of mardiness
Three litres of gaming
And a bag of Doritos
That would cheer me up

A football full of sportiness
Five tons of artiness
A green forest full of animals
One horseshoe covered in luck

Put in the oven for thirty minutes
Then let it cool.

Cassius M (10)
The Welbourn CE Primary School, Welbourn

Recipe For Happiness

50lb of gaming
70ml of cheesy pizza
100 litres of Krispy Kreme doughnuts
50lb of football
Three pinches of cheese and onion Pringles
700 litres of cuddly rabbits
70ml of greasy Domino's
Another KG of greasy doughnuts

First, add the cheesy pizza to a football match for an evening of paradise.
Next, add a tube of cheese Pringles to a hug with the rabbits for ultimate happiness.
Finally, add a box of Krispy Kreme doughnuts to an hour on Xbox for the most relaxed afternoon ever!

Joe Miller (10)
The Welbourn CE Primary School, Welbourn

Me And My Bike

I go cycling a lot
Even when it's boiling hot
In the cold or wet
But I never regret

In races, I compete
One day, I hope to be elite
Cycling, cycling, I love it so much
My handlebars I clutch

In the forest or on the road
Even when it's raining loads
On the pedals, I push down hard
When I leave my front yard

I go cycling with my dad
In my kit, I'm clad
I just want to thank him
Because of him, I love it to the brim.

Elise G (10)
The Welbourn CE Primary School, Welbourn

My Favourite Activity

Camping makes me happy
Camping makes me sad
Camping gives me excitement
Camping makes me mad

The best time to go camping
Is in summer when it's always warm
And good for walks

Camping by the lakes
Camping by the sea
Camping by mountains
Camping in fields

Camping makes me happy
Camping makes me sad
Camping gives me excitement
Camping makes me mad.

Evie Batchelor (10)
The Welbourn CE Primary School, Welbourn

This Is Me

My friends are very helpful and kind
They make me laugh
They help me with my maths

My friends are very nice and amazing people
And they are kind to me
I like to play with my friends
And watch YouTube.

Isla W (10)
The Welbourn CE Primary School, Welbourn

Favourite Activity

Biking is my favourite
Biking is the fastest
Biking is perfect
Biking is entertaining

The best time to bike
Is late afternoon
When the sun shines
On your solid helmet.

Maxi M (9)
The Welbourn CE Primary School, Welbourn

I Know A Girl

I know a girl who likes apples and cheese
I know a girl that likes climbing trees

I know a girl who likes doing the splits
I know a girl who loves doing craft kits

I know a girl who has two cats
I know a girl who likes wearing hats

I know a girl who wants a puppy to cuddle
I know a girl who gets in a muddle

I know a girl who likes pasta for tea
I know a girl and that girl is me.

Eliza Barford (8)
Totternhoe CE Academy, Totternhoe

This Is Me

T wo green eyes
H air colour is brown
I like horses and riding them
S inging songs

I don't care if I lose this competition
S weets and chocolate

M y favourite song is 'Bad Habits' by Ed Sheeran
E very day I read my reading book for school.

Holly Boiteux-Buchanan (8)
Totternhoe CE Academy, Totternhoe

The Things I Like

D arcey Bussell is who I want to be when I grow
up
E verybody is my friend, I like my friends
L oving and caring is what I like doing for my
family
P urple is my favourite colour, I like it so much
H aving a fun time
I 'm happy to help.

Delphi Joslyn-Walker (8)
Totternhoe CE Academy, Totternhoe

School Me

I go to school
And people say I look cool
Sometimes I mumble in class
But I mostly talk
And when I eat
I use my knife and fork
Four times tables take time
But I have never been in crime
I shine in the light
I also have a lot of might.

Madison Darvell (8)
Totternhoe CE Academy, Totternhoe

This Is Me

L oving
Y oung, eight years old
L ike nice friends
A nimals are the best
H appy

R ose all the time
O n time
S eem very pretty
E very food is nice.

Lylah Rose Nash (8)
Totternhoe CE Academy, Totternhoe

Carson

I can run really fast and that's no lie
I love to sing and dance and that's no lie
I help my mum in the kitchen and that's no lie
I care for Archie, Jeff's dog and that's no lie
I love to walk in the autumn leaves and that's
no lie
I can listen to stories well and that's no lie
I am Carson and I love my family
That is me.

Carson Rigby (7)

Worth Valley Primary School, Keighley

No Lies

I paint a lot and I am good at it
And that's no word of a lie!

I like going on a bus
And that's no word of a lie!

I love doing maths
And that's no word of a lie!

I love my family
And that's no word of a lie!

My name is Lucy
And that's no word of a lie!
That is me.

Lucie Gill (7)
Worth Valley Primary School, Keighley

That's No Lie

I love to see Bobby-May and that's no lie
I like to stare at the food when its cooking and
that's no lie
I like to wear nice clothes and that's no lie
I have three brothers and four sisters and that's
no lie
I like to learn new things and that's no lie
My name is Anne, that is me and that is not a lie.

Anne Roberts (7)
Worth Valley Primary School, Keighley

This Is Me

P is for perplexed
O is for oversleeps
P is for pleasure
P is for proud
I is for improvising
E is for entertain

J is for joker
A is for amazing
E is for exciting.

Poppie-Jae Antenbring (8)
Worth Valley Primary School, Keighley

Evah

E xciting stories
V isiting people
A mazing person
H appy girl

S uper sleeper
M iddle child
I nteresting hobbies
T elltale
H ungry smile.

Evah Smith (7)
Worth Valley Primary School, Keighley

This Is Me, Terrell

I like pizza and that's no lie
I'm an animal lover and that's no lie
Dogs are my favourite and that's no lie
I'm a professional Roblox player
But that is a lie
This is me, Terrell.

Terrell Howell (7)
Worth Valley Primary School, Keighley

This Is Me

I am loving and kind
I have a good mind
I get mad at my brother
And not any other
I have a pet fish
Who doesn't live in a dish
My favourite number is nine
This is Lucas.

Lucas Bogle (7)
Worth Valley Primary School, Keighley

This Is Me

A Batt who doesn't wear hats
Happy
Who treasure hunts
Watches Spider-Man
Plays Minecraft
Eats cheese crackers
Like to play outside
And finally
Loves all my family.

Joseph Batt (7)
Worth Valley Primary School, Keighley

This Is Me

T errific

H elpful

I ntelligent

S uper cool

I maginative

S uper cool

M ates with

E veryone!

Darcy Ingham (7)

Worth Valley Primary School, Keighley

This Is Me

M indful

Y ear Three

L egend

I ntelligent

E xtra funny

J oyful

A rgumentative

E xtra kind.

Mylie Jae Montgomery (7)

Worth Valley Primary School, Keighley

This Is Me - Elijah

I have red air
I sit and stare
I eat loads of cheese
I bend my knees
I like to joke
I try not to choke
And definitely don't like egg yolk.

Elijah Moorby-Byrne (7)
Worth Valley Primary School, Keighley

This Is Me

D iamond heart
Y elp for help
L ikes school trips
A ccurate work
N ature lover

And that's me, Dylan!

Dylan Richmond (7)

Worth Valley Primary School, Keighley

This Is Me

I wear glasses
I am so cheeky
I can be silly
I have four sisters
I have long hair
I don't like to share
That is me.

Keira-Jade Feather (7)
Worth Valley Primary School, Keighley

This Is Me

I am cheeky
I am sleepy
I eat all the time
I like to eat lime
I'm eight next month
This is me!

Jenson Greenwood (7)
Worth Valley Primary School, Keighley

YOUNG WRITERS INFORMATION

We hope you have enjoyed reading this book – and that you will continue to in the coming years.

If you're the parent or family member of an enthusiastic poet or story writer, do visit our website **www.youngwriters.co.uk/subscribe** and sign up to receive news, competitions, writing challenges and tips, activities and much, much more! There's lots to keep budding writers motivated!

If you would like to order further copies of this book, or any of our other titles, then please give us a call or order via your online account.

Young Writers
Remus House
Coltsfoot Drive
Peterborough
PE2 9BF
(01733) 890066
info@youngwriters.co.uk

Join in the conversation!
Tips, news, giveaways and much more!

 YoungWritersUK 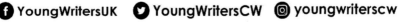 YoungWritersCW  youngwriterscw